SENECA

LEADERSHIP PROGRAMS

Pressed For Time Publications ©2005

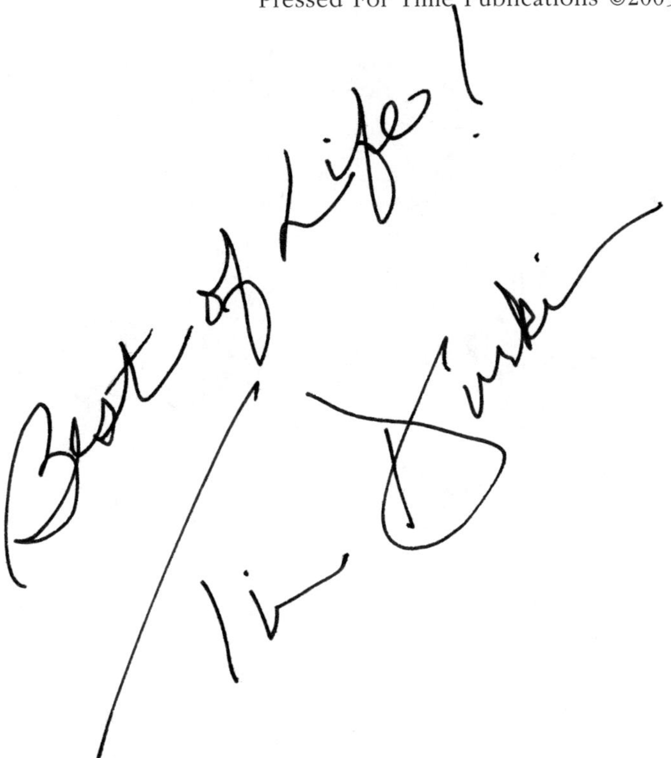

moving from PROMISE to PERFORMANCE

An Owner's Manual For Better Results

Tim Durkin

Seneca Leadership Programs

www.timdurkin.com

Pressed For Time Publications
18484 Preston Road
Suite 102 PMB 108
Dallas, Texas 75252

If you are interested in purchasing additional copies of *Moving From Promise to Performance. An Owner's Manual for Better Results,*
please contact:

Tim Durkin
972-250-4300 or 1-866-748-4300
or visit our website
www.timdurkin.com
Educational and quantity discounts available.

Moving From Promise to Performance. An Owner's Manual for Better Results.

Designed by Cathy John

Printed in the United States of America

ISBN: 0-9767092-0-1

To Elisabeth Reed Wagner
who had to leave early

Surely an angel walked among us.

contents:

moving from **PROMISE** to **PERFORMANCE**

using this book:

Don't read this book.

This book isn't for you to read; it's for you to use. It's an owner's manual, one focused on the most important vehicle of all—you. It is designed to give you the tools, tips and techniques you'll need to move from promise to performance.

Because it is an owner's manual, this book shouldn't be read in one sitting or in a linear fashion. Instead, read the chapters that cover topics of interest to you. If your meetings are running flat, for example, turn to Chapter 7 and learn how to make your next one more exciting and informative. Want to know when to be a leader? Then start with Chapter 1, "Lead or Manage". In short, skip ahead, jump around, and use the book as it best suits you.

Are you **ready to go to work?**

Many of the thousands of people who have attended my sessions have told me that, even though my topic was business, they discovered that the information was useful in their personal lives as well. This should really come as no surprise. Because work takes up so much of our time and energy, we now live blended—and hopefully, balanced—

lives. This book is organized with that truth in mind.

The first half of this book speaks to those professional topics that might also have some application in our personal lives. The second half targets our personal growth and development, yet also can help us in our professional lives. I hope you find both halves useful in getting better results in both your personal and professional endeavors.

This book is skinny, and it's skinny for a reason. Most people in today's world simply don't have the time to sit down and read a 12-pound tome on management. So this book was designed to be a quick read. And since I'm guessing that you're probably a pretty quick study anyway, you and this book should be a perfect match.

These chapters are **big ideas.**

You should also know that each chapter has been written to focus on one idea that, if used, will impact your life. These chapters are big ideas—game changers, if you will—but ones which pack an awesome punch.

Every chapter—even this one—ends with a Performance Summary, boiling down each idea into its purest actionable form. The key word, of course, is "actionable". If you always do what you've always done, you'll always get what you always got. And, as Einstein famously observed, "Insanity is doing the same thing over and over and expecting a different result."

I have a wise friend, George Knight, who once observed, "If you want to do things differently, you have to do things differently."

Sounds simple right? Perhaps, but do not confuse "simple" with "easy". The tools, tips and techniques outlined in these pages are effective beyond a doubt, but changing one's behavior is difficult at best. I encourage you to take the plunge, embrace and make some of the changes outlined herein, and see the positive impact they make. If you desire to move from promise to performance, then you have invested wisely.

PERFORMANCE:

Read the book's chapters in any order you desire, focusing on what catches your attention. Read one chapter a day if you like, but remember that this book is an owner's manual for your life—and you should always keep your owner's manuals handy.

Lead or Manage?

What's Right and When?

- **The choices are these:** Heat Light

- **Fill in the blanks:**

  Leaders provide ___________

  Managers provide___________

- **The answers:**

  Leaders provide Light.

  Managers provide Heat.

That's the difference between leading and managing, and a question I've been asked with regularity since taking the platform as a professional speaker and consultant nearly a dozen years ago.

Then, as now, the people who asked that question were seeking guidance in doing the right thing at the right time, not just an academic examination of linguistic difference. It seemed important to not only have a concise answer, but an answer that would serve as a template for a variety of situations.

Studying management and leadership has become an exercise in overwhelm. Googling two terms finds more than 175 million pages of information on the Web alone, and boiling down the collective thinking on when to lead and when to manage leaves us with a simple message. Today's successful managers should excel, first and foremost, in energy management.

Energy management is the key.

Whether we are in manufacturing or services, the manager's primary job is to manage his or her own energy as well the energy of the group. By applying the energy analogy again, it's easy to see the difference between making sure people do things right (managing) and making sure the right things are getting done (leading).

When we talk about managers and leaders, we aren't talking about two people. We are talking about one individual with two separate roles. In the role of leader, we provide direction, energy, vision and sometimes hope. As managers, we make things happen.

Sounds simple.

The real challenge, however, comes in knowing what to do when.

It's common for some people to rely on one role more than the other. Providing light doesn't always produce results. The same is true about heat. As someone once said, "man without a vision will perish." Maybe so, but if all man has is a vision, he's done for anyway.

Here's why. Results matter. In business, results are practically all that matters. Results lead to profits. Profits are to a business what breath is to a body.

The English philosopher John Ruskin once wrote: "What we think, what we say and what we believe is, in the end, of little consequence. The only thing that is of consequence is what we do." He's talking about results.

There are few things more energizing than operating when the so-called heat is on, but when the heat doesn't come off, energy is the casualty followed quickly by results. Why? Because providing heat for an extended period of time can wither the collective energy of a group or the individual radiating the heat.

Let's be realistic. Some people don't get it and never will no matter how much light you give them. Sometimes you have to move that halogen beam of yours close enough to singe arm hairs, just to get the group's attention. In neither the leadership or management roles should we ever sanction incompetence.

PERFORMANCE:

For those of you just starting out as managers or those who wish to examine their own balance of management and leadership, try this simple litmus test.

After an interaction with an individual or a group, ask yourself these two questions:

1. As a result of that interaction did that person(s) feel like I provided them light or heat?
2. Which was my intention to provide?

Hire for **Fire**

If there is a more important function for a manager than making good hiring decisions, I'm not sure what it is.

I am suggesting that all other things being equal, or nearly so, that it is far better to have ***ignorance on fire than brilliance on ice***.

My belief in this area is supported by experience, observations, and countless discussions with people who run successful operations. The consensus seems to be to ***hire attitude and train skills***. It's a lot less expensive and far less time-consuming to hire skills than to generate, or worse, regenerate attitude.

I am not implying that you should overlook or ignore all other character traits, skills, abilities, or intelligence and hire only the super-enthused. Nor am I suggesting hiring the top executives of your company based on their attitude alone.

How many times have you seen a supposed superstar from another company come in full of promise and a supposedly oil-gusher-like-producing Rolodex, only to fall short of expectations or even fail outright?

If you're a sports fan, you can easily call to mind how many superstar free agents fail to live up to their price and the expectations of their new teams. Then consider how many "walk-ons" excel.

Why do these so-called superstars fail? The reasons are probably many and varied, but the facts are clear: past performances carry no future guarantees. An indicator maybe, but not a guarantee.

On the other hand, look at the success rate when you hire a person with hair-on-fire enthusiasm. They seldom fail. They don't know what they don't know and they plow through what others find as obstacles. Their naivete is as refreshing as it is useful. And succeed or fail, they cost less.

The **mortgage rookie.**

Recently I met a young man, an unvarnished rookie, in the mortgage business. He had previously been the manager of the cafeteria in the building where the mortgage bank is located. He had served food to many loan officers, but knew little about the business. What he did know was that the successful loan officers were making far more money than he was and he was working at least twice as many hours. With a young family, a strong desire to better provide for them, and a fundamental belief that he could learn the business, he began to badger the executives in the company for a job when they visited his cafeteria.

Though he had no experience, he had the fire. As the insightful bank senior VP who hired him told me, "We needed people during this boom time and we rolled the dice with this young man." In his first year, a partial-one at that, he generated a nearly unheard of (even in boom times) $19+ million in loans in just nine months! When asked how he felt about his performance, he said it was a good start, but he could do much better. And he did.

What's the difference between a person like that and the person who turns in a mediocre performance despite experience and a so-called great Rolodex? Fire.

Keeper of the **flame.**

In medieval times, groups of people – sometimes entire villages – traveled over vast expanses of land. These groups would move during the day and camp during the night. Night brought cold and hunger. Consequently, it was important to get the fires burning quickly for cooking and for warmth.

Interspersed in the traveling group was a person who carried a small container of burning embers. This person's sole responsibility was to protect this fire-starting material. This person was, in fact, called "the keeper of the flame". It was as much a responsibility as it was an honor. With the keeper of the flame doing his/her job, fire was quickly available for the entire group. This idea has application even today.

Who are the keepers of the flame in your organization? Do you have one? It would be a very good idea to get one or to groom one.

PERFORMANCE:

It's better to have ignorance on fire than brilliance on ice. Hire attitude and train skills whenever possible.

chapter: 3

Pray for **Problems**

If you are now, or aspire to be, a manager, supervisor, or leader there is one thing you will need more than anything else—problems. If there are no problems, there is no need for you or for the position you occupy.

The message is: get excited about problems.

Problems are not now and will never be in short supply. So given an abundance of problems, what do you do with them?

First, try not to solve them. Let others solve them, if they can.

One of your primary tasks as a manager is the growth and development of the people who report to you, and problem-solving is one of the finest ways they can grow.

Please note that I am not advocating that you abdicate your position or your authority. If you give someone a problem to solve and they don't, the blame lands squarely on you. Not fair? Of course not, but it's true.

The best way to help others solve problems

is to teach them the difference between two words: ***blame*** and ***contribution***.

Blame and **contribution.**

If the person is looking to assign blame for the problem, it won't get fixed. What's worse, new processes to avoid similar problems in the future will not be established. Blame is guaranteed to keep perspective and attention in the past tense. You and your group should develop an allergic reaction to assigning blame.

Contribution, on the other hand, is essential in defining the root cause of a problem and then developing methods and procedures to prevent the same or similar problems from occurring again.

Contribution is fact-based analysis devoid of most emotion. Therefore, it is much more likely to get at the heart of the matter.

Another benefit of contribution is that it depersonalizes the source of the problem. If someone can be sure that the analysis of the problem is based on contribution rather than blame, it is far easier to accept personal culpability if it needs to be assigned.

Mistakes will be made. That's the good news. Problems are merely opportunities dressed in work clothes. That's even better news.

Is Apollo 13 famous for being another lunar voyage? No. It is famous for the way in which the crew on the ground and the crew in the spacecraft solved the numerous, vexing and life-threatening problems that confronted them during the flight. Had it not been for those problems, the world would barely remember Apollo 13. As it turns out, the problems and the solutions brought a great deal of attention to a space program that had slipped off the front pages, becoming another shining moment for NASA and the United States.

PERFORMANCE:

If you have people who report to you, let them solve the problems.

Never allow discussion about problems be about blame. No one can change the past. Blame is destructive. Encourage discussion about contribution. It is future-focused and points to areas we have more control over.

When the "they's" go away and the "we's" show up, progress is at hand.

chapter: 4

A **Complainer** is a **Gift**

Nobody likes a complainer, right? Wrong. I like them fine.

They can be very valuable. Here's why.

I have come to see a complaint as a statement of commitment.

When someone says they don't like something or that something is wrong, they actually are saying they support and believe the opposite. They are saying that there is something they believe in and/or value more. They are stating that they want something to happen that is different from what is happening currently. It's usually a good idea to listen. Some of the world's greatest ideas and achievements came from contrarians. Maybe all of them.

Suppose someone tells you that they don't like the new process because it's too time-consuming or a simply a waste of time. What they're really saying is they like the old way or some new version of the process. In fact, they are declaring they could commit to something else.

Hear complainers out. Then ask them to describe what they feel and how they could commit to another course of action or another way of thinking. Then see how you can work together to find some other way to get the job done.

I'm sure you're thinking, "I don't have time to listen to every complaint my staff can bring up" and you'd be right. You don't. I hear your complaint. The beauty of using this technique is you will quickly train your staff to present solutions, not problems. How would your job situation improve if you had a staff that was trained to bring you solutions instead of problems?

Here's how it may sound. "I don't like this new procedure and I think it would be more effective if we did this or that instead. Here's how I think it could be worked out."

Think of the industries and businesses built on the efforts of people dissatisfied with the status quo. Practically the entire information technology industry, from xerography and laptops to networking, came from minds of people viewed by some as malcontents.

Remember, when people don't complain, it

could be because they don't care, and that could be a huge sign of trouble.

If, on the other hand, they complain, but can't think of anything they want more, they're whining. Warn them. If they persist, make them go away. Complaints for the sake of complaining and without opposing commitment are viral. Allow them to fester in your organization at your peril.

Listen to the constructive malcontent. He/she may not be complaining but rather lobbying.

PERFORMANCE:

Train yourself to hear complaints as statements of commitment for a new and different way. This will raise your stature as a listener as well as a leader. Be sure to get the complainer to describe and, if necessary, defend their position. In the end you will have a staff of creators rather than complainers.

chapter: 5

Listen Up!

THE Essential Business Skill

A recent study by Loyola University sought to identify the single most critical skill that makes a manager effective. The number one skill was listening.

That isn't surprising when you consider we spend about 45% of our time listening, unless we are a manager or supervisor. Then the percentage jumps up to 55 %, unless we are a C-level person (CEO, CFO etc.) and then listening takes more than 85-95 percent of your time!

Think of your salary. Now figure 50 % of it and that's what your company is paying you per year just to listen. Are they getting their money's worth? Are you?

The purpose of this chapter is to make you aware of one important fact that everyone in business needs to know: If a message has emotional content for the listener, the listener has two physical reactions. First, they begin to go blind. Second, they immediately begin to experience anything from slight hearing impairment to complete deafness.

What you say. **What they hear.**

Who determines if a message has emotional content? The sender or the receiver? The answer is the receiver. In fact, the receiver determines the entire content of the message, emotional or otherwise. The meaning of the message is also found in the receiver.

It's important to remember that it doesn't matter what you said or what you meant. What matters is what they "heard".

Why is this important in **business?**

Let's take this simple scenario, which is being played out hundreds of times a day in the world of business. Suppose your manager speaks to you and wants you to take care of a situation she's noticed. She wants you to talk with an employee about a rather steep decline in their productivity. She instructs you, in no uncertain terms, to be open, honest, candid and, most of all, supportive. She also wants to make sure that you let the employee know they are valued and that you and even your boss stand behind them, ready to help in any way possible. Knowing that this is an uncomfortable position, she reminds you once again to be direct, candid and supportive.

You call the employee into your office and begin to discuss what you and your boss see as shortcomings and concerns with his performance. Candidly, but kindly, you mention that you and the boss stand ready to help him return to his previous high level of production.

After several minutes of this mostly one way conversation, you ask your employee if he understands. He nods his head and says, "Yes."

But did he?

Would it surprise you to find out that the performance of the employee not only didn't improve, but got worse? Or maybe that the employee left the company?

"How can this happen?" you ask yourself. He said he heard your promise of support and encouragement. But did he?

No, he didn't. He was momentarily "deaf". He was sitting there, thinking any one or more of a number of thoughts:

Maybe he was thinking:

"Uh oh. Time for me to dust off the ole resume… "

Or,

"This guy is such a jerk. I have the largest order this company has ever seen in my briefcase. I've been working on it for months and I can't wait to lay it on him and hear his apology."

Or,

"I've really messed up now. I've got to use all my time looking for another job because they're just being nice. What they are actually saying is, 'Go get another job before we have to fire you... and we are going to fire you.'"

Whatever is going on in his head, one thing is certain, he isn't listening. Yet when the manager asks if he understands what he has just said, of course he will say, "Yes." But did he? No.

Here's the problem. The manager will hold a person responsible for doing what he told them to do. Didn't they say they heard and understood? Yes, that's what they said, but they didn't actually hear the message. They were having a near-deaf experience.

The problems associated with poor listening are monumental in business today. So ask yourself, "What are the problems that poor listening is causing in my company or, for that matter, in my life?"

True Listening

Here is a process that I call ***True Listening***. This method can make any conversation more productive and respectful.

True Listening does not guarantee that both sides agree, but it does guarantee that both sides will respect and hear the other side. It also assures the relationship won't be fractured by poor listening skills or by each side merely waiting to talk instead of listening.

The **process:**

Dick and Jane are going to talk about something they know they totally disagree about. Yet both are very passionate about where they stand. The fact remains, however, that this topic has to be discussed. Knowing the incendiary nature of the topic, both agree to use the ***True Listening*** method.

Briefly stated, one person can't begin to make their point until and unless they can summarize what the other person has said to the other person's satisfaction.

1. One person states his or her view to the other.

2. The second person restates what they heard to the first person's satisfaction. Then the second person makes his point.

3. The first person then restates what the second person said to their satisfaction. And the first person makes his point.

4. This back and forth process continues through the entire conversation.

Does this process ensure satisfaction? Does it ensure that there will be a so-called winner and loser? Does it mean that one person will convince the other person to "see things their way"? Not necessarily.

This process ensures that each person knows they have been heard by the other. And it assures that respect and understanding will endure between the two parties

For ***True Listening*** to succeed, both sides have to know the rules and abide by them.

This process only takes a minute to explain and can yield a lifetime of improvement in those key relationships in your life.

PERFORMANCE:

Listening could be the biggest part of your job.

If you have any designs about being a leader, then developing excellent listening skills is an absolute requirement.

If you have a broken or damaged relationship, make sure you listen very closely the next time you interact with that particular person. Your efforts will be noticed and in all likelihood rewarded.

chapter: 6

Vigilance and Renewal:

The Price of Success

A mentor and I were reviewing the state of my business. He had just finished asking me if I was satisfied and if I wanted my business to continue to do well. I replied, "Sure."

Then he said, "Tim, if you do want to keep your work going well, then let me ask you a question. Do you know how to boil a frog?" It was one of the craziest questions I have ever been asked.

I laughed until I saw that he was serious, so I mumbled a lame reply about, "Well, I guess you throw it into boiling water."

"Wrong!" he said, "If you do that, the frog will jump right out every time."

How to **boil a frog.**

My friend went on to explain a lesson I will always remember.

"You see Tim, the way you boil a frog is to put him in room temperature water and then turn on the heat. The frog is fine at first, even enjoying his time in the water."

"However, as time goes on and the temperature rises, he becomes more and more drowsy and sluggish. He is unaware of the hot water (groan) he is in. If he does notice that the water is getting too hot, he no longer has the strength or the will to jump out. Then he's cooked."

Businesses are the same way. If we don't remain vigilant, if we don't remain alert, then sloppiness and self-satisfaction can creep in. We begin to settle for less. Worse, we become complacent and sluggish. We begin to sanction incompetence. Then we're cooked.

Good versus **great.**

Someone once said, "Good is the enemy of Great." I couldn't agree more.

"Great" is consistently performing the basic principles and patterns of success in an excellent manner.

"Great" is identifying and destroying the termites of high performance that cause us to be satisfied with "good".

"Great" is keeping "the eye of the tiger".

"Great" is the expectation and execution of excellence.

The moment we let our guard down, "good" raises its ugly, mediocre head. "Good" is insidious. "Good" is relentless. To make matters worse, we are not usually the ones who discover that we have settled for being "good". It is our customers. They notice first. If we are real lucky, they will bring it to our attention. However, studies show they usually stop doing business with us and talk about our slippage to others. Sloppiness doesn't leap, it creeps.

A lesson from an icon.

A wonderful example of this was brought to my attention by Stanley Marcus, the late icon of fashion and retailing, and generally accepted arbiter of exquisite taste. At the opening dinner of INFOMART, an information technology market place in Dallas, Texas, I had the true honor of sitting next to "Mr. Stanley".

Ever gracious, he was fascinated by the architecture of the building, which was a duplication of the Crystal Palace in London, the site of the very first World's Fair. With near childlike wonder and excitement he looked up and around the arching lobby and foyer. All of us who worked on the project for the previous two years were nearly exhausted, but immensely proud and excited from the rush to the grand opening of this unique project.

As Mr. Stanley politely peppered me with questions about the history and design of the building, he humbly shared with me his encyclopedic knowledge of London. Suddenly he turned to me and asked, "So, Tim, when are you going to begin to repaint?"

With the smell of the days, if not hours-old, fresh paint in my nose, I replied, "Mr. Stanley, I certainly hope it will be at least a few years before we have to face that task."

Then, he gently put his hand on my arm, looked at me with a friendly face, eyes twinkling and calmly said, "Wrong answer, Tim."

As my face flushed with embarrassment of having obviously flunked a pop quiz by a legend, I managed to stammer, "Ahhh, okay, when do you think we should start repainting, Mr. Stanley?"

"Well, tomorrow of course. Do you know why, Tim?"

"No sir," I replied.

"Because you must always have a spirit of renewal in your projects as well as your life.

If your customers notice that your building needs painting, then you have failed to renew it. And then you have failed your customers, yourself and the owners. Remember that, Tim."

I have and I always will.

Hopefully, now you will, too.

Thank you, Mr. Stanley. Rest in peace, friend.

PERFORMANCE:

Look around. See where "good" has crept in to replace "great" in your business or personal life.

In most organizations, it's easy to spot if you look around with fresh eyes. If you see "good," treat it like a termite and exterminate it with "great".

chapter: 7

One Thing That Will **Make Meetings Matter**

No one I know likes meetings.

How often are you in a productive one? Isn't the main reason for meeting to get something done? How many times have the results of meetings you attended been another meeting? In my world, planning another meeting is, perhaps, the greatest waste of meeting time.

We have all left a meeting, saying something like, "Well, that was a complete waste of time." Or, "Why did we have that meeting again?"

So, what's the big problem with meetings today? Is the problem with meetings a poor agenda or the lack of one entirely? Or, is it because it was led improperly?

Can or **can't?**

It was once my pleasure to work for Mr. Trammell Crow. He is, without a doubt, one of the most famous names and forces in residential and commercial real estate. And he is also a fine gentleman.

In the span of about ten seconds, he changed my practice of meeting management completely. There has seldom been a non-productive meeting on my calendar since. This also includes meetings I have attended and not led.

Here's what he did.

There was a group of about twelve people meeting about one of our projects. All the Crow organizations attract people of high intelligence, strong opinions and high energy, so I can truthfully say there were no shrinking violets in that group.

The meeting had gone on way beyond its useful life span and feelings were pretty frayed. Yet some individuals were determined to get a certain outcome. Others at the table were just as determined to get something different.

You can easily imagine the kind of discussion, or should I say percussion, going on in that room as the proverbial "dead horses" were beaten again and again.

Mr. Crow walked in and silently took a seat

in the back. It was not unusual for him to come into any meeting at anytime. Usually his presence caused people to sit up a little straighter and at least appear to be more attentive. Yet this time the air was charged with ego and personality.

As he quietly surveyed the room, it took him less than a minute to size up the situation. After just a few more seconds, he leaned forward and said, "Excuse me. I'm sorry that I got here late (remember he wasn't invited), but I just have one quick question. Is this a ***can*** meeting or is this a ***can't*** meeting? Because if it's a ***can*** meeting I can stay. If it's a ***can't*** meeting I've got better things to do."

The silence was palpable. As the air began to circulate once more, someone mumbled something about getting back on track. But everyone knew that, in the instant of that remark, the focus shifted from negative to positive.

Since that day, I periodically take a few seconds to survey the meeting room from the "Mr. Crow position" and ask myself and then the group, "Is this a ***can*** meeting or a ***can't*** meeting?" I've seen nothing more effective for bringing focus to problem resolution and/or action planning and accountability than those nine words. Try it yourself.

After hearing me tell this story, one of my staff started bringing a tin can to meetings. She would place it in the center of the conference table and when things got off track, she would quietly reach over, lift it up and then set it down just loud enough for everyone to notice. Wordlessly, the meeting got refocused.

Another tip for keeping meetings focused: Have the chairs removed (and maybe even the table) from the meeting room. Nothing like the physical pain of standing until business is concluded to help everyone stay on track and keep the outcomes crisp.

PERFORMANCE:

Each meeting develops a tone of its own as it moves forward. Become aware of the tone by mentally stepping away from it and determine if it is developing a *can* tone or a *can't* tone. Publish your findings to the group.

chapter: 8

If You Miss the Target, Don't Blame the Target

Setting Goals, Targets, Objectives & Intentions

A short story:*

"Could you tell me please which way I ought to go from here?" asked Alice.
"That depends a good deal on where you want to go," said the Cat.
"I don't much care where," said Alice.
"Then it doesn't matter which way you go," said the Cat.

Many people live their lives like Alice. If you do and want to change, this is a good chapter for you.

The lesson in this is simple, but very important. All intentions, outcomes, goals, targets, and objectives must be stated in the ***positive***. But more about that later.

First, whether you decide to call it a goal, objective, target, or outcome, you need to

*From ***Through The Looking Glass and What Alice Found There*** also known as ***Alice In Wonderland*** by Lewis Carroll.

make sure that you ***have*** them. Many people don't. Instead they careen through their lives like Alice, never quite knowing where they're going, but hoping for the best.

I am surprised at how few people actually have goals and how fewer still actually write them down.

There is a reason to write, and I mean handwrite, your goals. The process of writing bridges the gap between the conscious and the subconscious.

Simply having goals and writing them down puts you in that small percentage of achievers who actually get the results they want. Writing down what you want out of life is a lot better than careening through it, hoping, praying, and knocking on wood for the best.

Goals for play versus **goals for pay.**

Ask yourself how willing would you be to spend upwards of $50.00 per round if the golf course had no greens and no holes? If you were going bowling, would you pay for a game in which no pins were set? If you are into shooting sports, would you be interested in not having any targets? Would you like to play basketball without any baskets or tennis without any court lines?

Of course not.

Here we have an interesting situation. We are insistent about having targets and goals in our play time, but many of us aren't at all insistent on having goals or targets in our work time.

When I ask my clients and colleagues what their goals are, I often get answers like, "We want to improve customer satisfaction", or "We want to gain market share", or "I want to get a new product rolled out".

These statements are not goals. They are processes.

A goal has to have metrics. A goal has to include specifics like: do what, by when, by whom, and by how much.

Having a **target.**

> "If the archer misses the target, it is not the target's fault."
>
> –Ancient Japanese Saying

Creating a target before you shoot will let you know how you are doing and, more importantly, how you can do better. If you miss it, at least you know what you were aiming at and by how much you missed. More importantly, you'll come away knowing how much you need to adjust in order to hit the target when you try again. You were planning to try again, weren't you?

A goal without a deadline is just a wish. Timeframes add urgency to any activity. Thus, timeframes are excellent at focusing energy, and energy devoted to a task is called "work".

As we discussed earlier, a goal has to be stated in the positive. State what you want to have happen, not what you don't want to have happen, or what you wish to avoid. Would you be more inspired by a statement that says, "You want to improve profit by eight percent," or by a statement like, "I want to reduce losses by eight percent?"

Setting goals is not something only big companies do. In fact, it is more important for small companies and entrepreneurs to set goals in order to have a clearer financial picture of their business.

Most small companies or individuals would be unable to endure more than a few months or quarters of losses, so having goals and knowing performance-against-goals can give you a snapshot of the health of your business. More importantly, this very important data will show trends. The world of business shows up in trends, some short, some long, but trends are the way of business.

NLP Goal Setting.

Perhaps the most complete analysis and methodology for setting goals comes from the world of Neuro-Linguistic Programming (NLP).

NLP is described as ***the study of the modeling and application of human excellence.***

Outcome setting in NLP is very powerful and the process is easy to explain but more difficult to execute. However, the time spent setting outcomes thoughtfully and carefully will be immensely helpful toward achieving your important goals.

The **Process:**

Positive

Make sure your goal is stated and described in the positive.

Specific

Imagine the outcome as specifically as possible and answer the questions: who, what, where, when and/or how.

Have you broken the goal into small enough "chunks"?

Proof

How will you know when you have it?

Think of what it will be like to have it, using all of your senses.

Resources

Do you have everything you need to achieve it or do you need additional resources?

Is achieving the goal within your control or is it dependent on other people or different circumstances?

Size

Is the goal the right size?

Is it too small to excite you or so big as to overwhelm you?

Do you need to "chunk" it down to smaller-sized outcomes or "chunk it up" to inspire and stretch you?

Ecology

This part is very important. Most people never think about the ramifications of achieving their goals. We are almost never the same after achieving important goals. That is usually, though not always, good. The ecology frame is critical for outcome forming.

Ask yourself:
What would happen if I got it?
Who else does this affect?
Is this goal right for all circumstances in my life?
What will achieving this goal cause me to loose?
Does it respect your health, relationships and that of others?

Act
What will be your first step? Take it!

Sound simple? It is. Jack Welch of General Electric fame said, "Simple is seldom easy". Never confuse simple with easy. Simple is elegant and, therefore, seldom easy to attain without purposeful thought and action.

PERFORMANCE:

Set just one goal using the NLP model and see what happens. Only through experience will you truly be able to understand the power of clear goal setting. Remember, few people actually do this, so if you do, you stand to benefit enormously.

chapter: 9

The Secret to Attaining and Maintaining High Performance:

The Feedback Model

Have you ever wondered why great athletes are able to perform and sustain such high levels of performance? Perhaps you just assumed it is because they have so many physical and mental gifts that it's easy for them to maintain peak performance. If that's what you assumed, you would be wrong.

At the elite level of sport, there isn't that much difference in the physical and mental gifts of top performers. For example, the difference in stroke average (the effective "batting average" of professional golfers) of the PGA Men's tour participants between number one and number fifty on the ranking list is much less than a single stroke. At the elite level of high performance differences in ability can be quite small indeed. That's why on any given day anyone can win.

There is something else that top performers do all the time. And by "top performers",

I also mean outside of sports as in business, entertainment or medicine. What they practice is a technique that you can learn and do very easily. While you may not win a major championship you will see a dramatic improvement in your performance.

The great thing about this technique is that it's something that you can easily do. It requires very little effort, just a commitment. It will make a big difference in your performance almost immediately. In fact, if you do nothing else in this book except this, you can change your life in a positive way. Yes, this idea is worth thousands of times what you spent for this book, if you use it.

The Breakfast of **champions.**

The one thing that top performers do that the rest of us usually don't is to seek feedback on a continuing basis. You could say top performers are insatiably hungry for feedback.

Feedback is not to be confused with so-called "constructive criticism". There is no such thing as "constructive criticism". The root word of "criticize" actually means "to rip or tear flesh".

The *Constructive Criticism* Model

Recall a time when someone, probably someone you reported to, told you: "Hey (insert your name here), would you like some constructive criticism about what you just did?" The truth is you would prefer a root canal to this so-called character-building event. You more or less have to say, "Sure".

Then he starts …

"Well (insert your name here again), I liked this and I liked that and I thought this went very well and then out it comes … the dreaded pause followed by the single most annoying word in all the work place—"but". Or perhaps they may try to soften it up a little and use "however", which is just a bigger "but".

Then it's all down hill after that. You're thinking, "Now he's going to say what he really wanted to say all along." Or, "Okay here it comes…." By any stretch of the imagination one thing is becoming crystal clear. You are on your way to the woodshed.

The **Feedback** Model

Thankfully, there is a far more productive model, a proven way to improve performance. This model is elegantly simple and is often dismissed as too simplistic. However, its simplicity is one of the reasons it works so well. It is called ***The Feedback Model***.

I'd like to thank my friend Alan Fine, founder of InsideOut Development, for teaching me this technique. Alan is a PGA coach and was one of the coaches who helped the European Ryder Cup team come from behind and beat the American team on the final day of competition in 2003.

The Feedback Model consists of following three questions:

1. What worked?
2. Where did you get stuck?
3. What will you do differently next time?

Technically, there is a fourth question: "what else?" This is asked after each of the three questions. "What else?" serves to encourage the performer to think about all facets of his or her performance, not just the major good things or the big flaws that easily come to mind.

Perhaps the best way to look at this process is through an example.

Suppose you have an employee named Kim

who works for you. She has just finished a project that met your expectations and then some. Yet, there were some areas that you feel less than enthusiastic about regarding her attention to some details. You feel the same about the way she tried to "go it alone" much of the time, failing to ask for help when it was clearly needed.

This is an ideal time for feedback. It's soon after the completion of the project so most of the details are fresh in her mind. Feedback is always more effective the closer to the event that it occurs. That is one of the reasons traditional annual review and feedback sessions are insanely ineffective or maybe just insane.

The process begins with you approaching or calling an employee who works for you whose name is Kim and saying, "Kim, I have some feedback for you on the ABC project. Would you like to hear it now or can we schedule some time soon for a brief meeting on it?"

Be assured the first time you do this, Kim will not hear feedback. Instead, she will hear ***constructive criticism***. Consequently, your request will be treated with something less than enthusiasm. This will be true even if Kim thinks she did a stellar job.

Kim replies, "I guess so. I'm free to talk now if you are."

What **worked?**

Move into a private area and then say something like, "So Kim, before I tell you my view on how things went, please tell me from your standpoint, what worked?"
There it is, the first question: ***what worked?***

Then listen. Remember listening is the highest compliment you can pay another individual, especially if that person reports to you (or lives with you, for that matter). You will be very tempted to talk. Don't. You will have your chance, but if you keep quiet and listen, chances are you will learn some very interesting and possibly surprising things. Then ask the fourth question, "What else?"

Keep asking "what else?" over and over as you help your colleague build as long a list as possible. Remember to make sure they keep listing the positives. Do not be surprised if many people tend to shade into areas they feel didn't go well or, because of their previous long history with so-called constructive criticism, they feel you are going to bring up anyway.

Always bring them back with a comment like, "Let's not get into the other stuff. I'd like to talk about what worked first." The idea is to get them to make as long a list as possible and exhaust every single positive thing that happened.

Where did you get **stuck?**

Next, ask question number two: where did you get stuck? Be careful here. The question is not, "What didn't work?" The question is based on accountability. It asks, "Where did YOU get stuck?"

You don't want to hear that the spike in interest rates shut off spending or that Mercury went into retrograde before Venus could get aligned with Mars. Even if those statements are true and contributory, the idea is to keep the person focused on what they can control. Again the question, "What else?" should be asked repeatedly.

Let me point out again that keeping your mouth shut at this time is perhaps the hardest part of the process, but do it anyway. Listen, listen and listen again.

The reason you must listen is because, by now, the person senses something very different is going on and even if they don't know why or what, they have a strong feeling that the conversation is going well.

What would you **do differently?**

After they have finished their list, ask them the final question: what would you do differently? This question underscores the primary reason, perhaps the only reason, you are using feedback anyway.

When you cut right through everything else, the only legitimate reason to give someone feedback is to ***improve performance***. Improve it next time, next week, next project, or tomorrow. This question is designed to get your colleagues thinking about how to do it better the next time, how to formulate a plan. It guides them to review lessons learned and how to apply them.

This is the key to ***The Feedback Model***. It's all about the growth and development of the other person. And at this point in the conversation, they can probably sense it.

It's **your turn.**

Having asked the three questions, now it's finally your turn. All you need to do is answer the three questions yourself with some minor changes.

To the first question state, "I think this worked and this worked and I agree that this went well." If you have an opportunity to give the person some recognition, kudos or sincere and deserved praise, then, by all means, do it now.

Many studies have shown that a primary motivation for working and trying to do a good job is "psychic income," also known as praise and recognition. It doesn't spend but it definitely earns interest.

Next, move on to where you feel they got stuck. Be honest. If you must point out a shortcoming or failure, please remember to ***criticize the performance, never the performer***. Be hard on the issue but soft on the person. Anything that smacks of personal attack will cause the other person to stop listening and get defensive. Unfortunately, you may not be able to know if this is happening, despite sitting right across the table from them.

It's far better to say, "Expenses are still too high compared to investment and return." Don't say "You still don't have expenses under control." If you make your comments personal, then you make them deaf and it's almost impossible to help anyone to whom you have given a near-deaf experience.

Finally, you get a chance to review their plans during the ***do things differently*** section.

You may or may not agree with their plans or ideas. It's not important, as far as the model is concerned, if you agree or disagree. If you are their manager, you certainly have a right and perhaps an obligation to voice your thoughts about their plans. Most importantly, however, you want to be sure they have a plan. Then, you decide together how you can best support them and their plans. In fact, an excellent question to ask at this time is, "How can I best support you at this time?"

Why it works.

I mentioned earlier that the purpose of feedback is to improve performance. People are more likely to improve performance if the words for improving performance come from their mouths and go to their ears, instead of journeying from our mouth to their ears.

Neil Rackham of Huthwaite Research found, conclusively, that people are motivated to action when ***they*** express the need to act. The best ways to express needs are to either write them down or voice them. Consequently, the effectiveness of this feedback model is because it is an "ask" model, not a "tell" model. It allows the person responsible for improving performance to declare their intention after reviewing what they felt was good and bad about their performance.

Another reason the model works as an "ask model" is because it forces the manager to listen. The highest compliment you can pay another person is to listen to them. Listening is also the number one most admired trait of an effective leader.

In this scenario, we have discussed how managers or supervisors can use ***The Feedback Model*** effectively. The model works very well in peer-to-peer discussions. Suppose you see a colleague or a friend whom you know to be working on a big project. You might casually ask her or him how things are going. Then you might ask them what's working, where are they getting stuck, etc.

Obviously they have no reporting relationship with you, but this technique gives them a chance to quickly assess, in an organized way, how they are doing.

You may or may not have something to add when it's your turn to state the three questions back to them, but the important part in peer-to-peer feedback is to get their input.

Interestingly, it is even possible to have feedback sessions with people thousands of miles away who didn't even witness your work. All they have to do is ask the three questions.

I often get feedback from someone who has not seen my work in years and is located more than a thousand miles away when we have the feedback session. Why does it work this way? Because ***The Feedback Model*** is basically positive and organized self-talk.

Give yourself some quiet time daily, weekly or whenever appropriate and ask yourself the three questions: What worked? Where did you get stuck? What would you do differently?

Be objective and honest.

PERFORMANCE:

Try this powerful model for improving performance today. Use it on yourself. Incorporate it into your daily routine. Set up your own experiment. Try it with some members of your group or family. Then examine the results.

This process really works. Why do you suppose the great athletes and the great teams and performers use it all the time? How good do you think any professional team would be if they only got the coach's feedback once or twice a season?

chapter: 10

It's Not WHAT you Say to Yourself That Makes a Difference: It's What You Repeat

The mind is a wondrous and sometimes funny thing. Take, for example, the scientific fact that our minds cannot distinguish between something that it vividly imagined and something that actually happens.

Does this sound hard to believe? Try this classic experiment.

Think of a large, yellow, very juicy, lemon slice. Capture it clearly in your mind and then imagine biting into it. If you are like most people and have vividly imagined the lemon, you will have gotten a response such as increased activity of your salivary glands. Some people may even get that small shiver after imagining the tartness of the lemony taste. While you really didn't bite into a lemon, your mind told your body that you did and your body reacted to the message from your brain.

So what does this have to do with your future? Just this. Be careful what you say to yourself. You're body doesn't really have much of a sense of humor. It doesn't know when you're "just kidding" or teasing. It reacts to your thoughts. It always thinks you mean what you say. It does not detect sarcasm. Your body takes your mind and what you think very literally and very seriously.

Good book. **Great idea.**

I enjoy books and read voraciously since my travel schedule usually gives me plenty of both airport and airplane time. One of the most influential and amazing books that I have ever read is ***As A Man Thinketh***, by James Allen. This book is at least 100 years old, but its message is as current today as it ever was.

This book is published in a variety of formats and should cost around five dollars. Yet it is almost priceless in its insight and inspiration. My copy resides on my nightstand next to the book of my faith. I travel with a copy at all times. Mr. Allen wrote in the tone and tenor of his era, so at times reading his style of writing is a little unfamiliar. Yet, because there is such laser-like insight in his words, it often takes two or three readings to comprehend the simplicity of his expression.

Yes, I realize that the last sentence seems

contradictory, but buy the book and see if you agree.

Here is an excerpt:

"A man's mind might be likened to a garden, which may be intelligently cultivated or allowed to run wild; but whether cultivated or neglected, it must, and will, bring forth. If no useful seed are put into it, then an abundance of useless weed-seeds will fall therein, and will continue to produce their own kind."

This passage will reward closer examination and re-reading.

There is no other book I can consistently depend on to make me feel better or more excited about life than this one. And there is another bonus when you read this book. Depending on the printing format, the entire volume is only seventy pages.

Your **self talk.**

The lesson of this chapter is to be exceedingly careful of your self-talk. You are not just mumbling to yourself, you are programming yourself. An important point to remember is that your mind is a perfect instrument. Because it is perfect, it cannot process a negative thought into a positive action. In fact, your mind cannot process negatives at all.

Want proof? Try this. **Do not** think of a lemon. Now, **do not** think of the color blue or any shade of blue from sky to light and from powder blue to deep royal or navy blue. Now, **do not** think of a large purple elephant standing knee high in orange grass spewing a rainbow out of its trunk.

Notice how good you are at thinking about stuff you were told not to think about? It's a little scary actually. Remember, whatever you want, whatever your goal, target, or outcome is that you desire, make sure that you state it in **positive** terms.

Say, think, or write, "I will make an excellent presentation this morning," or "I will hold everyone's attention and everyone will understand the information I am conveying."

This is much different than thinking to yourself, "Whatever you do, don't mess up today because the boss is in the audience!" Guess what you will do after your brain naturally edits out the negative word "don't"? The irony about our self-talk is that when we speak in the negative, we actually manifest whatever we wish to avoid.

We've all heard about the power of affirmations and many of us use them. Hopefully they are all positive. However, we can just as easily affirm negative as well as positive thoughts.

When you say things to yourself or others such as:

"I am no good in the morning."
"I just can't speak before a group of people."
"I always lose my car keys."
"I'm never on time."

Statements like these are negative affirmations and consequently, you will manifest your own negative reality.

PERFORMANCE:

Test yourself and pay close attention to your self-talk for just one day. See how many times you have negative conversations with yourself. Notice how often you repeat them.

Changing your self-talk will help you get better results as much as anything else we talk about in this book. Combining positive self-talk with richly defined outcomes, goals and objectives is extremely powerful.

chapter: 11

The Worst Word
in the world

There is a word that is so toxic, so malignant and so destructive, that I am asking you to banish this word from your vocabulary immediately.

I assure you that each time you use this word with someone, you hurt them and negatively affect both their performance and their desire.

So what could this word possibly be? Most people say "can't". It is not "can't".

I'm not going to make you guess. Just remember this, NEVER tell anyone what they "SHOULD'VE" done.

There are three reasons why:

1. ***Should've*** has a unique ability to make people feel defensive. They think to themselves, "Whaddya mean what I SHOULD have done? Like this jerk could do any better? Like he could handle my workload? Like he could even spell 'MBA'?" Making people defensive turns them deaf and makes them angry.

2. ***Should've*** is tied to, attached to, and inexorably linked to the concept of failure. You are, in fact, telling someone "You should've and you didn't, ergo you failed". Saying or even implying such a thing is hardly a way to build someone up.

3. ***Should've*** is past tense. What can you do about the past? Exactly nothing. No one can do anything about what they ***should've*** done. As the ancient Greek dramatist Agathon reminds us, "This alone is denied the gods, the power to undo the past."

With that one little word you are directly telling a person, "I know you're feeling defensive. You are, indeed, a published failure, and there is nothing you can do about it!" Why don't you be sure and add, "Have a nice day!"

The **good word(s).**

So if ***should've*** is the bad word, what is the good word?

The good word is actually two good words: **next time.**

You can always replace ***should've*** with ***next time***, as in "next time try this," "next time do this," "next time think about something else." Next time...next time...next time....

Next time contains no judgment and is future-focused. And future is a time frame we can control.

Interestingly, I have rarely heard a person, performing at the professional level, say the word ***should've***. I hear ***next time*** frequently, but ***should've*** almost never. Listen to professionals being interviewed and hear their language. Then listen to your own.

Who else?

While we are on the subject of not telling anyone what they ***should've*** done, let's expand our definition of ***anyone***.

It's pretty obvious that it's never a good idea to tell a spouse, boy/girlfriend or significant other what they ***should've*** done. It probably isn't too difficult to think back to an argument or disagreement that contained or even began with this word. Probably didn't go too well, huh?

However, there is one group of special people in our lives when the temptation to get "shouldy" with is overwhelming—and that group is our children.

Why, if this word is so destructive, are we so tempted to use it with the treasures of our lives? Ironically, it is because we love them so much.

We are eager to help them become complete, totally successful and happy people. Who knows exactly what that will take? You guessed it! That would be us.

After all, what was the sense of making all those mistakes if we couldn't tell someone about them? Besides they're stuck there in the passenger seat of the SUV for twenty minutes on the way home from the soccer game. They can't get away.

So we tell them, "You should've passed the ball over to Mary. She was standing in front of an open goal doing deep nasal probes while you're over there, trying to evade three defenders by your lonesome."

Or, "You know, you should've spent more time on math and less time on IMing your friends and you would have got into State U the first time you applied." Or, "You should've spent more time on those scales and exercises and you wouldn't have forgotten them during the recital."

While we think we are loving them, that kind

of love from the most important person in their world feels pretty "shouldy".

Next time **say next time.**

Try ***next time***. As in, "***Next time***, try to look for an open person." Better yet, how about, "What would you do next time you had the ball and three defenders were close to you and someone might be open near the goal?"

On the subject of not getting "shouldy", there is one person you must NEVER, EVER, get "shouldy" with. Know who? That's right. YOU!

But do we? Absolutely! We say things to ourselves that we would knock someone into next week if they dared say the same to us. What's worse, we don't just get down on ourselves, we get waaaay down on ourselves. We catastrophize, awfulize and horriblize our own mistakes and shortfalls.

We say things like, "I should've handled that meeting very differently... but did I? Oooh noooo! I messed it up real good, I would've had to work really hard to mess it up anymore...and isn't that just like me to mess up a meeting that meant so much... course it is and, will you look at that, in the mirror oh great! My hair has neither body nor shine…oh my, this day was a complete waste of make-up!"

"Pretty soon the way things are going I'll be living underneath the viaduct where Central Expressway crosses the Interstate. What will I live in? Oh, probably some refrigerator box I'll manage to find and what will happen? Probably the first night I'm there, someone will want it and kick me out!!! Oh, I should've handled that meeting differently."

Many of us have a problem with these pessimistic explanatory styles and we need to disrupt such thought patterns as soon as we notice them. We also need to be careful not to get "shouldy" with ourselves.

PERFORMANCE:

Replace the words ***should've*** with ***next time*** and see what happens to the conversation. You'll be pleased to find that the results are positive.

chapter: 12

Overcoming Limitations:

A Lesson From Cows

Everyone knows that cows aren't very close to the top of the intellectual ladder. So imagine my surprise when I discovered that I was acting like a cow when it came to reaching my goals. Chances are in some ways, you probably are too.

Let me explain.

Shortly after moving to Texas, I was invited to a friend's ranch. It was, to use the common parlance, "a big spread".

My friend invited me to share in the chore of checking on his herd in the afternoon. We scrambled into his pickup and set off across the rolling hills of brush, live oak and mesquite trees. Soon we were passing through one fence line and then another. I noticed that we did not have to stop to open or close gates, but instead went over asphalt strips with lines painted across them.

Being curious, I asked my friend how the cows stayed in the right pasture.

"It's because of those cattle guards we keep going over," he replied. Then, sensing my confusion, he explained that early ranchers had to erect gates around all the pastures on their property. While it was effective at keeping the cows in, it was a nuisance for the ranchers. Every time they reached a gate, they had to stop the truck, climb out, open it, secure it after going through, get back in the truck and repeat the process on the other side. Doing this over and over at every gate in the hot Texas sun or the cold, windy winter day was a chore in itself.

He went on to explain that some smart rancher took the gates off, dug a shallow ditch, and laid 10 or so six-inch diameter pipes across the opening. While cows are not long on analysis, they do know they can't walk across pipes with their hooves. The problem with the pipes, the rancher explained, was that the ranch hands often hit them at about forty miles an hour, causing all sort of untoward things to happen to expensive ranch vehicles. Soon, those high vehicle repair bills caused ranchers to look for another solution to keeping the cows fenced. Finally, some upstart rancher came up with an effective technique to keep the cows where they belonged. This ingenious rancher picked up the pipes, filled in the trench, paved over the dirt with a little asphalt, and painted ten lines across the area where the pipes had been. Sure enough, whenever the bovine wanderers reached that spot, they eyed the lines suspiciously, knew they couldn't go across them, and ambled back to do their cow thing.

"They never figured out it was only paint!" my host chortled, "and if you talk to my cattle, please don't tell 'em," he added with a wink and a sly grin.

What are your **cattle guards?**

This experience got me thinking. What are my painted cattle guards? What are the self-imposed limitations that keep me from doing what I want?

It wasn't hard to come up with some answers. I dislike flying. I am an introvert. Yet I make my living speaking and training groups of people all around the country. How do I manage these apparent conflicts?

While I don't like to fly, I love to read, so rather than think about hovering over the Earth at 35,000 feet, I think of the wonderful opportunity I have to read. And rather than thinking that I'm speaking in front of a large group, I maintain eye contact with one person at a time, since it's much easier for me to speak to one or a few than to many.

What are your painted cattle guards? What are the irrational fears that keep you confined and away from what you want to do, what you want to contribute, what you want to have?

The only fears a human being is born with are the fear of loud noises and the fear of falling. Every other fear is learned and can, therefore, be unlearned.

So what's it going to be for you? A life of adventure and accomplishment or a life limited by imaginary and self-imposed cattle guards and fences?

PERFORMANCE:

Examine your results and ask yourself if you are getting what you want. If not, could it be due to self imposed limitations? Perhaps you are acting like a cow.

chapter: 13

You can **Make (or Be)** the **Difference**

Long ago when large ships loaded with trade goods sailed the seven seas, things were different. Virtually all commerce between the so-called "old" and "new" worlds depended on the capacity and frequency of ships laden with trade goods.

Building sound ships was a practice that had been mastered. Steering them had not.

Since hydraulics had yet to be invented, ropes made from hemp and pulled on by men controlled the ship's rudder. In those days, ships could not grow in size to accommodate the need for more cargo space because the hemp and the steering mechanisms were not strong enough to turn the rudder. The force of the water over the size of the rudder defeated the strength of the hemp rope.

Eventually, some valedictorian of the time figured out a solution by sawing off at least one sixth of the rudder and reattaching it with hinges. This smaller section could easily be controlled. By turning this smaller section, the pressure on the rudder was reduced. In essence, he had created a rudder for a rudder. The correct term for this device is "trim tab".

If you want to see a modern application of this principle, look at an airplane or a boat. Steering and navigation during flight, sailing, and power boating are all made possible by utilizing smaller controlling surfaces attached to larger ones.

Your **rudder power.**

So what does this all mean for you? How many times do we have the power to control everything in an organization or group?

The honest answer is probably "seldom if ever". How many times do we have an opportunity to influence the direction of the group or organization? The answer is "often".

Realize that you can be a rudder for a rudder. Look for opportunities to help craft the course or the direction of your organization.

This idea is so powerful that the great R. Buckminster Fuller* has inscribed on his headstone: "Call Me Trim Tab".

As he explained:

"Something hit me very hard once as I was thinking about what one little man could do. Think of the Queen Mary—the whole ship goes by and then comes the rudder. And there's a tiny thing on the edge of the rudder called a trim tab. It's a miniature rudder. Just moving that little trim tab builds a low pressure that pulls the rudder around. Takes almost no effort at all. So I said that the little individual can be a trim tab. Society thinks it's going right by you or that it's left you altogether. But if you're doing dynamic things mentally, the fact is that you can just put your foot out, like that, and the whole big ship of state is going to go. So I said: Call me Trim Tab."

*Excerpted from R. Buckminster Fuller tape transcript interview with Barry Farrell, February 1972.

PERFORMANCE:

Remember the great quote of Mahatma Gandhi who exhorted us to be the change we wish to create. Quit pointing out how things would be better if those at the top "got it" and be that which you wish to see in others. Be a "trim tab". People will notice and your field of play will expand over time.

chapter: 14

A **Personality Profile** that Actually Works

You've probably read about the personality profiles designed to help us work with others more effectively.

Over the years, we've all become familiar with many personality profiles, beginning with Myers-Briggs and going on to DISC and Hartmann, to name a few. They all sounded good, but the problem was trying to use them effectively.

You had to be a memory expert to apply the knowledge gleaned from them. While all the profiles make sense intuitively, they are cumbersome and confusing to use effectively when we're trying to sell something to someone, help someone with their goals, or work with someone more effectively.

When my friend Dan Coates and I were discussing this problem, he shared his four-part personality model that is easy to use, easy to remember, and helpful when we are dealing with others. In short, he came up with a "bare bones" approach for understanding people.

Them Bones

According to Dan, when there is work to be done and you need the help of others to get it done, there really are only four types of people at your disposal.

Knucklebones

Knucklebones are people who are always punching holes in ideas and telling you how things can't be done and why. Usually short of cynical (though not always), they are essentially negative, but could be just unsure of themselves. They may have a cloud over their heads or maybe they weren't held too often as babies. Don't get me wrong, a little dissent is a very good thing. It inoculates the group from the dreaded groupthink condition that brought us the "O" ring and Watergate disasters.

Dissent is okay, but not as a steady diet. As I have said elsewhere in this book, I think complainers are valuable unless complaining is all they do. Dealing with knucklebones is easy. Listen to them. Take them for what they are. Weigh the merits of their argument and move on. Or make them move on.

Overcome your desire to ask them if they would like some cheese with that whine. They get their validation through airtime.

Jawbones

Jawbones are people who talks a good game but little else. They approaches every problem with an open mouth.

Here we have another talker who likes to say the first thing that comes to his/her mind, which often isn't much. Jawbones resist action as it pushes back their accountability. Or in some people, they actually fear failure or success. Who really knows? Recognize them by their airtime consumption which is often off-topic. They are broadcasting when they should be tuning in.

Handle these people by having an agenda and a strong meeting leader who will thank them for their contributions and then ask for other viewpoints.

Wishbones

Wishbones are sideline stalwarts, frequently hoping and wishing, but lacking action. Full of hope and wildly optimistic, they are usually unable to marshal the energy needed to do something. Wishbones are often stuck in the past, looking back and lamenting the roads not taken or actually avoided because they were unpaved.

Sometimes mistaken for a knucklebone, wishbones are different because they actually want to do something, but lack focus or have too much inertia to DO anything. Wishbones often come with a ready set of excuses that are often proffered before they are needed.

Handle wishbones carefully as they mean well. They hope for the best and will be the first on the bandwagon when things go well. When things don't work out, they will not engage in "I told you so", that's the purview of the knucklebone. Instead, the wishbone will have one more item for their wish lists and they'll actually be happy in a perverse sort of way. Share victories with wishbones. They are your most vigorous high-fivers.

Backbones

Finally, there are the **backbones**, the people who get it done, whatever it is. You definitely want these people. If only they came with labels to make it easier to spot them early. They are driven by results. And if you aren't driving like they want you to, they may grab the wheel.

Keep backbones challenged or you won't keep them at all. Recognition is less important than what they learn from the work or nature of the challenge. Get as many backbones on your assignment as possible.

A good way to recognize backbones is to remember that little kid who sat on the baseball bench. He never took his glove off. Instead, he popped it while imploring, "Put me in coach, put me in!" Look for the glove poppers in your organization and then put them in.

PERFORMANCE:

Evaluate the personalities you have in your group or organization using this model. Share this model with them and ask them to put themselves in one of the categories. Even without asking them where they rated themselves you will have raised their awareness to their own behavior.

Sometimes raising awareness is all it takes to get better results from someone. In fact, without an awareness of how a person is actually perceived by self and others, a person in all likelihood cannot change.

chapter: 15

The **Four Stages** of Our Lives

When he was asked how he managed so much reform and progress in just the first two years of his presidential term, Woodrow Wilson said matter-of-factly: "I use all the brains that I have got and all that I can borrow." It was good advice then and still is now, and it's advice that I have personally taken to heart.

I was reminded of those words when I had the pleasure of listening to Naomi Rhode, a legend in the speaking profession, speak in Dallas a few years ago. Near the end of another one of her usual brilliant and provocative sessions, Naomi went on to explain that we have four stages of life which she described as: student, success, significance and servant.

Naomi pointed out that she was taking Wilson's advice to heart by drawing on the work of Bob Buford, author of the book ***Half Time***, regarding these stages.

The **student stage.**

During the ***student stage***, we learn skills necessary to get by and to perform in our jobs or our roles as a parent, spouse etc. During this stage, we are alert for tips and techniques for improving our lot in life or that of our loved ones.

It's a good idea to always keep one foot in the student stage. You have probably heard the adage, "If you're not green and growing, you're ripe and rotting."

By way of example, I was astounded to once observe the legendary Zig Ziglar attend a training class at the National Speakers Association annual convention. He went to the front of the room and feverishly took notes throughout the session. He asked questions and then thanked the presenter (who was more than slightly surprised) for teaching him so much.

I later discovered that this is standard procedure for this Zig. He never stops being a student. Impressive.

The **success stage.**

After the student stage, we reach the ***success stage***. During success, we basically make it.

We learn our job skills and hopefully we succeed as partners, parents, providers and/or professionals. Our goal during this stage is the accumulation of wealth and wisdom. Then something interesting happens. Many of us discover that we can succeed and still feel somewhat dissatisfied, maybe even a little empty. That's a sure sign we're ready for the next stage

The **significance stage.**

Having succeeded at one level, we began to search for significance. The formula for significance is very simple: GIVE BACK.

You aren't under any obligation, moral or otherwise, to give back as some would have you believe. Perhaps you think the financial flow through the service you provided, the company you created or the jobs you provided is enough. Maybe it is. But nature abhors a vacuum and when you create a vacuum by giving something away, nature will rush to fill it up again. That's why tithing works. Giving away is a sustaining behavior. Not giving away is a limiting one.

The **servant stage.**

The fourth stage of life and perhaps the most important one is service or the ***servant stage***.

Once you realize that all the money and stuff in the world will not guarantee your happiness, you can begin to make a difference through service. I have never met a person who gave back and was unhappy. This is especially true if their service involved more than writing a check.

If their service involved working on the food line of a homeless shelter, visiting the sick, building a home with Habitat for Humanity, etc., they enjoyed it. Through experience and observation of others, I do not believe it possible to serve others and be unhappy. You won't have a bad day if you helped someone else have a good one.

Take a simple test: find a homeless shelter in your area and serve a meal. Go to a nursing home and ask to see someone who doesn't get any visitors. Go to a hospital and volunteer. Sign up to be a "hugger" at a Special Olympics event in your area. If you aren't happy, you'll at least be grateful. I'm betting on the happy.

Student. Success. Significance. Service. And the easiest of these to perform is service. No one can begin to tell you how to serve. You have to find that out for yourself. Look around. Someone needs your help, and as you help others, you will discover the secret of true leadership. To serve is to lead.

PERFORMANCE:

Start serving and find out you can work the equation backward. Through your service, you find greater significance and then you can reach success beyond your expectations. Thank you, Naomi and Bob.

chapter: 16

Make a **Living.** Make a **Life.** Make a **Difference.**

We all want to do three things: make a living, make a life and make a difference.

The question is how?

The answers are infinite and depend on our individual circumstances. But one thing is clear. We can do all three if we maintain balance and examine our progress on a daily basis in each area.

How do we do that? Two ways:

1. Think about things
2. Don't think about things.

For twenty minutes every day, close your door or leave your office or find a quiet place and think. Just think. Even if it feels like just a short period of time. Don't answer emails, phones or take interruptions in any way. Be selfish about this time. Think about the three areas: make a living, make a life and make a difference.

Make a **living.**

Now, think about how you are making a living. Are you working to prove yourself or are you working to express yourself? Are you preparing for the next promotion or are you concentrating on what needs to be done now? Examine your work life and the direction it and you are taking. Are you meeting your goals? If not, what can and must you change?

Make a **life.**

Next, think about how your life is going. Remember when people talked about seeking life balance and we discovered that, with laptops, cell phones, beepers and Blackberrys, the best we could hope for would be life-blending? Life balance is elusive. Life blend seems here to stay.

So, the next question is how is your blend? What would those around you say about your blend? Are you enjoying yourself? Are you seeking happiness but settling for pleasure? What kind of shape are you in physically, mentally, spiritually and emotionally?

Daily assessments aren't selfish, they are self-interested.

Ever notice when you board an airplane,

they always go through those directions that say, "In the unlikely event of an emergency, a mask will drop down in front of you. If you are seated with a child (or someone who is acting like a child) please fix your mask first and then help the other person with theirs."

This is a great piece of wisdom. It underlines the importance of taking care of yourself first before you can be expected to be of any value to someone else.

Make a **difference.**

Taking time to examine how you are making a difference is also important. I have often heard the statement, "To whom much is given, much is asked."

Frankly I don't think we, as humans, have a true moral imperative to help another person, at least not before we help ourselves. I think it's very unhealthy to help others at the expense of not helping ourselves. Let me add that while there is no true obligation to help one another, there are amazingly bountiful, if intangible, rewards for doing so. Notice how I put helping others after taking care of yourself and those around you. There is nothing inherently wrong with acting with enlightened self-interest.

The reward for helping others is mostly intrinsic, though it has been the author's experience that helping others has generated an amazing amount of compensation, both tangible and intangible.

The **candle flame.**

There is a story about a candle that I would like to share with you. You see I can take my candle and use it to light yours. My candle flame is in no way harmed by this action and yet we have now doubled the amount of light. You can then take your lit candle and light someone else's. I'm sure you get the picture. Helping others never hurts us, yet we are always making a difference.

You never really know how much good you are doing when you give back. My favorite expression is "Anyone can count the number of seeds in one tomato, yet no one can count the number of tomatoes in one seed."

Clear your **mind.**

I have come to the conclusion that it is important to take twenty minutes every day and NOT think. That's right, spend at least twenty minutes each day in undisturbed solitude and meditate, or if you prefer, pray. The act of clearing one's mind is not only refreshing and relaxing, but also energizing and restoring.

Despite the widely known and generally accepted knowledge of the benefits of meditation, only a small percentage of people actually do it. Everyone can come up with many excuses but few, if any, seem valid.

The simple fact, backed up by a great deal of medical research, is that there is real value in meditation or if you prefer, quiet contemplative prayer. Taking just twenty minutes out of your day to do this is a small price to pay for the benefits you can reap. This practice renews, refreshes, restores, and re-energizes you for the rest of the day. It is time invested not just time spent.

Think you can't afford twenty minutes a day for this? Then your schedule is probably out of control and you may want to spend time reordering priorities and put a healthier, more productive and happier you at the top of your list.

PERFORMANCE:

Take the time, as outlined above, for ten days and see if you don't get a heightened energy level, clearer perspective and improved performance in all three areas of your life.

A **final word.**

"It shall come to pass" is written 465 times in the Bible. "It shall come to stay" is never written even once.

So how do we make ***it*** stay?

We make ***it*** stay through use.

This book is full of practical and proven ideas that, if used, will improve your results. What is required by you is a commitment to the performance suggestions at the end of each chapter.

Experts have suggested that it takes between seventeen and twenty one repetitions to make an action or thought a habit. Whatever the number is, it is most certainly more than one or two.

So the final performance of this manual is to pick one or two ideas that resonate with you and repeat them until you notice that they become habitual. After seeing your desired results you will be convinced that everything you have read in these pages works.

RESOURCES

As A Man Thinketh by Robert Allen

The Servant as Leader by Robert Greenleaf

The 7 Habits of Highly Effective People by Stephen Covey

Man's Search For Meaning by Viktor Frankl

The Life You Imagine by Derek Jeter

Learned Optimism by Martin Seligman Ph.D.

Critical Path by R. Buckminster Fuller

Journey to Center by Thomas Crum

Introducing Neuro-Linguistic Programming by Joseph O'Connor

What to Say When You Talk To Yourself by Shad Helmstetter Ph.D.

Shut Up, Stop Whining, and Get a Life by Larry Winget

The Sedona Method by Hale Dwoskin

Class Acts by Mary Mitchell

The Miracle of Mindfulness by Thich Nhat Hanh

The Path of Least Resistance by Robert Fritz

Raise the Bar by Mike Vance

ACKNOWLEDGEMENTS

Whoever said that writing is a solitary pursuit never tried to write a book.

The list of people I wish to acknowledge could easily become a chapter by itself. Yet, I am sure I will forget or overlook someone along the way. To you I apologize even before I begin.

I start by thanking all the authors and experts I have read or encountered thus far, for your fingerprints are all over this book. I hope I attributed correctly, or at the very least, did you proud. Next, I want to thank my clients and business colleagues for your example, inspiration and guidance. Specifically, I wish to thank Stephen Covey for seeing something in me that I could not see myself and showing me how to access and use it. Also, a big thanks to Alan Fine, friend and former business partner, which is better than the other way around.

To Lucy Billingsley who gave me a chance to grow as no other person I know and for standing by me when I needed a friend when things looked pretty bleak. My success is owed more to you than I could ever repay. You started this whole thing Lucy and I thank you for it.

On the subject of irreparable debts the two people at the top of that list are Chick and Dianne Young. And they know what it's for. "Thanks" is way too small a word for what you helped me do.

Special thanks to my clients who have shown confidence

and courage in hiring me over the years. I hope I added value. A partial list includes Marcia Maxwell, Ken Johnson, Bill Long, Chuck Tonkin, Chrissi Rhea, Dave Witt, Tom Durel, Gayle Consiglio, Edna Bruel, Larry Schunder, Kathie Baikie, Rick Kneipper, and Mark Hardwick, Trish Trimble and Bill Winsor (the best boss I ever had). A quick and sincere thanks to Lindsay Wehner and Lori Lux for all your ongoing support.

Another big thanks goes to the Big Chillers, my sanity support group up in Michigan.

I can't forget to thank Mike Vance, a friend, a mentor and an inspiration. Thanks also to Lee Colan, who was relentless in checking up on my progress in the writing of this book. We were in a race to see who got their book out first. I only lost by three years.

To my friends and colleagues in the National Speakers Association especially Christine Cashen, Max Jaffe, Mike Hoffman and Gary Rifkin. To Kathy Reed, Rod Monahan, Nancy Stuckey and Paula Elerick your friendship is inspiring. Thank you for telling me what I needed to hear instead of what I wanted to hear.

To Maureen for all the years of support and for being a great mom to our children.

A special thanks to Alice Adams, my editor. Perhaps interpreter would be a better word. Thank you for your patience and your gifts. If my voice seems strident or preachy it is because of my energy, enthusiasm and excitement about these effective ideas. Please don't blame her. Ralph Strand gets all the credit for the correct spelling and punctuation. Thanks Ralph, you are a true gentleman. Huge thanks to Geoff Owens, aka the word wizard.

To Mike and Ann, for the countless Saturday morning breakfasts where you were my sanity check, my reality check, and you picked up the check. To my sister Pat, I know you are my biggest fan, did you know I am yours?

To Cathy John, an amazing talent; a wonderful designer and more wonderful friend.

A special thank you to Susan Kellams, an early believer and tireless supporter. To "Mom" and "Dad" Finlay, for opening your hearts and your home to me. And to Jody, the best fantasy league player on the planet. Thanks for all the lottery tickets bro, but I won the day I met you.

To young Isabella Annsley, newly minted granddaughter and true gift, the personification of lightening in a body.

Finally to my children Shannon, Mike, and Colleen, who taught me everything I know about the amazing joy that is being a father and about life, living and making a difference. Thanks for growing up and being my best friends too. My pride is exceeded only by my love.

This book is self published and all errors and omissions are my own. For I am a learner as well as a teacher.

NOTES:

NOTES:

NOTES:

about the author:

Tim Durkin is President of Seneca Leadership Programs, a company dedicated to helping organizations achieve better results. Tim is a speaker, workshop leader, and consultant whose trademark high-energy approach has been sought after by some of the world's leading companies. With over twenty five years of successful hands-on industry experience Tim brings insight, energy, and solutions to problems at all levels of a company.

His client list includes GE, Ford, Exxon Mobil, Dell, GM, Alcon Labs, TGI Friday's, Ernst & Young, KPMG, IBM, Sun Microsystems, PHNS, Bank of America, SunTrust, and many others.

Always engaging, energetic and insightful, Tim's speeches and workshop sessions have been called life-changing events by many attendees. More important is that each session is crammed with practical ideas, tips, tools, and techniques that can help nearly anyone move from promise to performance.

Learn how Tim can help you and your organization get better results by calling him at: 972-250-4300 or e-mail: ***tim@timdurkin.com***